Praise for Speaker's Trifecta

Kristi Bramlett is the real deal. She brings the kind of wisdom that's not just learned, but lived, rooted in deep experience, grounded in grace, and carried with a fierce commitment to helping communicators become more fully themselves. Her insights on embodiment, authenticity, and presence have the power to change not just how we speak, but how we show up. I'm genuinely grateful for her work and voice.

— *Ian Simkins,*
Lead pastor, The Bridge Church

The Speaker's Trifecta is one of those rare books that offers both practical insight and deep soul work for communicators. As someone who's trained and coached hundreds of leaders – especially women navigating ministry and leadership spaces – I know how easy it is to focus only on content while missing the deeper alignment that true influence requires. What I love about this book is Kristi doesn't just teach you how to speak, she walks you into the why beneath your message. This book is filled with language and tools to align your mind, body, and soul in a way that brings integrity, clarity, and purpose to your voice. If you're a leader, preacher, speaker, or communicator in any setting – especially in the Church – this book will sharpen your thinking and deepen your impact. I'll be recommending it to every leader I know!

— *Kadi Cole*
Leadership Consultant, Executive Coach, Speaker,
Author of Developing Female Leaders and
Find Your Leadership Voice

Over my 30 years as a professional speaker, I've seen countless people attempt to coach others on the art of communication.

Yet, I've never encountered anyone who understands it—or teaches it—quite like Kristi Bramlett. She brings to communication what I've come to know as the deeper essence of integrity: being whole, integrated, and truly connected. Her brilliance shines through every page of this book. Any communicator who not only absorbs the rich insights Kristi shares but chooses to make them a way of being will find themselves more authentic, more impactful, and more fully alive every time they speak.

> — *John G. Blumberg*
> *National Speaker and Author of "Return On Integrity"*

In a world saturated with communication advice that treats speakers like robots to be programmed, Kristi Bramlett offers something revolutionary: permission to be authentically human. *"The Speaker's Trifecta"* isn't just another public speaking manual, it's a masterclass in embodied communication that will transform how you connect with others. Bramlett's unique background as both movement analyst and communication coach shines through every page, offering insights you simply won't find elsewhere. Whether you're delivering a boardroom presentation, teaching a class, or speaking from a stage, this book will help you move beyond being a "talking head" to becoming a fully integrated communicator. *The Speaker's Trifecta* is essential reading for anyone who wants their voice to carry the full weight of their humanity

> – *Shawn Williams*
> *Senior Pastor, Willow Creek Church*

From the moment I sat in one of Kristi's classes, I knew this was something incredibly special. Her ability to connect communication with mindful movement is powerful, practical, and deeply needed in today's noisy world. I've been speaking and leading for over twenty years, and I've learned more from Kristi about intentional, embodied communication than I've from any workshop, book, or course I've taken. *The Speaker's Trifecta* isn't just a book—it's a breakthrough. It's for anyone who leads teams, teaches, stands on stages, or wants to communicate with more impact and authenticity. This is a resource every communicator needs in their toolkit.

— *Melissa Mashburn*
CEO, Ministry Chick Network

The Speaker's Trifecta - Mind, Body, Soul is a masterclass in embodied communication. Kristi Bramlett brilliantly bridges the gap between what we say and how we say it — inviting speakers to shed performance-based habits, reclaim their physical presence, and show up authentically in every space they inhabit. Rooted in years of experience as a movement coach, Kristi offers practical insights that help communicators move beyond surface delivery into soul-connected communication that connects deeply with our audience. This book is a must-read for anyone who desires to speak with greater clarity, credibility, and confidence. *The Speakers Trifecta* is the book you didn't know you were waiting for."

— *Cheryl Nembhard*
TV Host, Global Speaker, Executive Director -Women Speakers Collective

Kristi coached us in person, and we still carry with us a checklist of insights to review before we give talks! *The Speaker's Trifecta* gives everyone the opportunity to benefit from Kristi's experience, wisdom, and insight. This is a practical, inspiring, and enjoyable book - have your highlighter in hand, there is gold in here!

— *Alex & Hannah Absalom*
Dandelion Resourcing

THE SPEAKER'S TRIFECTA:
Mind, Body, Soul

The Speaker's Trifecta:
Mind, Body, Soul

Kristi Bramlett

Minerva Rising Press

Glen Ellyn

Copyright © 2025 Kristi Bramlett

All rights reserved. No part of this book may be reproduced in any form or by any electronic or mechanical means, including information storage and retrieval systems, without permission in writing from the publisher, except by reviewers who may quote brief passages in a review. This a work of fiction. Any references to historical events, real people, or real locals are fictitious.

ISBN 978-1-950811-24-3

Cover image by Anna Louise Bramlett

Printed and bound in USA
First Printing November 2025

Published by Minerva Rising Press
864 Western Avenue
Glen Ellyn, IL 60137
www.minervarising.com

Introduction

1 | Embodying Your Content, Mind, Body, and Soul	7
2 | You Don't Know What You Don't Know	16
3 | All Movement Has Meaning	27
4 | Claiming Your Space	33
5 | If You Aren't Connected You Won't Connect	43
6 | Breath as Impulse	52
7 | Practicing Presence Connects the Mind, Body, and Soul	63
8 | Movement in the "Box"	73
9 | The Trifecta for Connected Communicators	79

INTRODUCTION

"There is nothing to prove and nothing to protect. I am who I am and it's enough."
— Fr. Richard Rohr

It all started years ago when I volunteered to work on a team at my church to determine if staff or key volunteers might be ready to teach in various positions. A vibrant, well-dressed woman entered the space where we were holding teaching team assessments. At the time I didn't know her too well, but she was completely at ease as she chatted with other people in the room. To be fair, the space always feels a little weird before an assessment. The speakers are nervous, and even the observers feel a bit of imposter syndrome as they seek to give helpful feedback. But iron sharpens iron, and that is exactly what happens in these moments of assessment. The confident woman settled in and began her talk.

Her talk was concise, she had a strong grasp on the material, and she seemed to have a deep connection to the content. She believed what she was saying. However, when she spoke, there were many unintentional movements that were distracting and didn't do anything to support her message. What I observed was a body that was disconnected from her mind and soul. After the assessment, we chatted a bit more about my observations and I offered her some extra movement coaching on the side. She was hungry to get better at the craft of communicating, and her excitement made me eager to help. We began talking about her excessive unconscious body movements that were "leaking out" when she spoke. I didn't tell her what to do or not to do, but we worked on exercises that allowed her to integrate authentic, intentional movement into her communication practice, and use the stage space effectively.

Communication is more than just speaking the words you have written; it is about delivering those words with your mind, body, and soul. It requires all three working in tandem - a triple threat, or "trifecta," of authentic communication. The more I worked with communicators, the more I realized that it is not just the stage presence that matters. Speakers must authentically communicate with every part of their being in order to convey their message effectively.

My path has been a wild ride, taking me from figure skater to actor, comedian, academic, movement analyst, and now, a coach for communicators. Each career shift built upon the previous one, equipping me with life experience and knowledge to create *Kristi Coaches Communicators*. As a movement coach, these are my objectives: to help speakers embrace their authentic selves in voice and body; encourage them to remove "masks they have borrowed" by emulating other communicators; lead them to use breath as an impulse for movement; give them permission to take up space without apology; and direct them to embody their content authentically. Over the last 15 years I have been organizing and codifying my coaching practices in the classroom with my theatre students, and with my communicator clients. What I have discovered is how similar and how applicable my practices for theatre students are to the new speakers I was coaching.

I was teaching my acting students to know who they were in voice and body, to create an empathetically embodied character, based on the given circumstances of the play or screenplay. They were to look at what the character had been through in their life that marked and shaped them into who we see on stage. As I watched my students over the years, I noticed a perplexing trend. Despite their efforts to learn lines and develop the character's emotional life, they often neglected to consider the character's voice, body, and movement. Because they weren't considering the voice and movement of the character they were playing, we ended up seeing more of the actor and their habits. We saw an actor working very hard, pushing to show the audience how emotionally connected they were to their character. This left us with two-dimensional characters whose minds were only being used to memorize lines and learn blocking. They would push (sometimes too hard) for an emotional connection to what their characters had been through, but their mind/soul understanding was not transferring down into the bodies of their characters.

These same challenges also emerged when working with my speaking clients. The speakers fell into one of two categories. First, some communicators relied entirely on "instinct" without making deliberate choices for movement, which lead to random gestures, wandering on stage, and verbal filler words causing them to lose momentum in their presentation. Others created a "public speaking character" with canned gestures and a "put on" voice. Their affected movement resulted in a disconnection from their authentic selves, not allowing them to connect with their audiences. Without understanding who they were in their own voice and body, they defaulted to ingrained habits, obstructing authentic, embodied communication. It became evident that my communicators were not making conscious choices about using their speaking space, choosing their movement, or engaging with their audience. As a result, they defaulted to personal habits, just like my acting students. We have all witnessed these traits in speakers we've seen in many different capacities, but few have sought to get to the root of these challenges.

The Speaker's Trifecta is for anyone who wants to understand what it is like to communicate authentically with their whole self: mind, body, and soul. I have witnessed significant strides in my clients' communication skills through the principles found in *The Speaker's Trifecta*. But these principles go way beyond a speaker's uses. This book will also benefit anyone seeking stronger self-awareness, communicating in sales or employee product education, for example. Any communicator who desires to make a stronger impact when presenting content will find this book a valuable resource.

Most available books on speaking or communicating are prescriptive. They might tell you what to do, how to stand, and how to gesture, but don't consider the speaker's preferences or what is authentic to them as communicators. As a movement coach, my approach to supporting communicators is reversed. It's essential to start with the speaker because we often wear "masks" in hope of becoming who others want us to be, rather than embracing who we are. In my work, the speaker discovers their unique movement preferences. They begin from a neutral, honest place, with minimal affectation, and craft a communication process that works for them. I don't tell them how they should move or gesture, or suggest they emulate other communicators. Instead, I focus on their unique preferences, affirm their intrinsic value, and encourage them to step into their true selves as communicators.

Additional pain points for communicators were revealed in 2020 and the years following the pandemic when Zoom sessions instantly turned us into "talking heads" on our laptops and smartphone screens. We were becoming even more disconnected from each other and ourselves. If people received any training on how to deliver embodied presentations in person, it went out the window during this time. And for the speaker that had no training in delivery, they were having even more trouble knowing how to be authentic in digital spaces. They were never trained in how to use their whole self when delivering content in person, so they had no context on how to embody their content online. As a result, these communicators were working twice as hard to make an impact in their field. They were struggling to close deals with clients, not getting the promised promotion. During this time, these speakers were either unaware that they weren't connecting or they had a keen sense of the problems but didn't have the knowledge of how to make changes they knew to be necessary.

The Speakers Trifecta offers a new perspective on communication. It's a journey to knowing that you are enough, with all your experiences and unique qualities. In fact, there is no one else like you in the whole world. And it is time to embrace your authentic self.

Instead of borrowing tricks from other speakers, focus on who you were created to be and how you can use the space around you effectively to support your message. Remember, authentic communication requires engaging your whole self: mind, body, and soul. Be curious about your process as a communicator. Be open to learning new things about yourself that will allow you to be more authentic. I'm excited to be working through *The Speaker's Trifecta* together. Let's Move!

1
Embodying Your Content, Mind, Body, and Soul

"Handwriting is more connected to the movement of the heart."
— Natalie Goldberg, *Writing Down the Bones: Freeing the Writer Within*

When it comes to creating content, it seems that the high demand for "interesting" communication has led to everyone trying to outdo everyone else on social media, making things bigger, better, and slicker than the person before them. Our culture is obsessed with production—how fast, how polished, how well-received, and how unique it can be in order to get views. But this fixation on the curated final product can prevent us from fully engaging with the process. I've even seen this with my acting students. When a student is cast in a role, they often focus solely on the opening night performance, skipping over the creative process that brings a character to life. They rush through the steps, quickly highlighting and memorizing their lines without deeply considering the character's backstory and how their life experiences shape their movements, posture, voice, and gesture. If they took more time to explore, research, and allow their imagination to roam, their performance would be richer and more authentic.

The only cure for these challenges is to completely shut down the impulses the social media-centric product brings. Put down the phone—slow down, think about what you are trying to communicate. Take your time, allowing your imagination to come to life during the process. Be present, undistracted by the world's noise. If an idea stirs something in you, jot it down and sit with it for a while. If you encounter something that piques your curiosity, hold onto it and let it evolve. Give your ideas time to marinate, allow them to settle, reflect on them for a day or two. How do these thoughts apply to your life, work, belief system, or relationships? Let the ideas roll around in your mind until they become clearer. Sometimes, I take an idea with me on a walk, letting it interact with my thoughts and feelings while I am moving. The process will take time, but will prove to be worth it in the end.

Developing content organically requires patience (something I personally struggle with), but it's essential that you aren't rushing the process. The goal is to get your ideas down, whether through voice texts, journaling, writing, or vlogging. You can sift through the details later. I often draw from Natalie Goldberg's free-writing process from her book *Writing Down the Bones* and have adapted it for my own work. During each free-writing session, I benefit from a prompt to help me focus my writing. The prompt for my writing session can be a word, an image, an idea, a piece of art, or a quote that I find interesting. I also set a timer for the length of time that

I will write. When I started the free-writing practice, I began with five minutes and gradually increased the writing time over several months. The most important thing to remember is that free-writing should flow—don't overthink, judge it, or self edit. Here are some of the rules I have adapted from *Writing Down the Bones* for my own free-writing practice:

1. Focus on your breath to connect your mind and body.

2. During the free-write keep your hand moving as you write stream-of-consciousness style. Let the prompt take you where it will. Sometimes it will take you in a new and surprising direction.

3. If you get stuck, write the last word on the page over and over until a new idea surfaces.

4. Avoid self-editing. Don't worry about grammar, spelling, or punctuation—your first instinct has the most energy.

5. You don't need to write on the lines, write on angles, in circles. I often use journals without lines to encourage more flexibility in my thinking.

Using free-writing for content creation is a great first step towards embodying your words with your whole self. I encourage people to approach their writing process with a mindset of curiosity to learn something new. When communicators are genuinely eager to learn as they begin writing, it fuels their passion for the subject matter, leading them to create content that is dynamically powerful.

As you free-write, notice how you move the pen across the paper, paying attention to what is happening with the levels of tension in your body. Take notice of how you are breathing: are you breathing with ease, taking deep breaths, shallow breaths, or are you holding your breath? As you write, are you weeping, smiling, or laughing? Does free-writing on a particular prompt bring you joy, or is there a knot in your stomach? Paying attention to how your body reacts during your writing process can give you some insight into how your audience might feel as they hear you speak. Your understanding of how your body is feeling during a free-write allows you to connect to something deeper as you write. Taking your ideas (mind and soul) and bringing them into visible form with your body is embodiment.

Once you've explored your ideas through free-writing, it's time to shape your thoughts into a story with a clear beginning, middle, and end. Claim the theme that you're trying to communicate to your listeners. It also might be nice to identify some takeaways from your content. Now we are moving into the crafting phase as you put all of your content together. Don't rush the process. Take as long as necessary. There's always more to discover as you refine your thoughts. However, make sure you complete the writing several days before you are required to present. Once you have your thoughts in order, research the content you are referencing to make sure the information is based in fact.

I love the free-writing process for creating content but I

would also challenge you to mix up your process every now and then. It will keep your ideas fresh. Changing things up might also keep you from feeling stuck in a rut. Experiment with different practices for content development. As a speaker, your task is to find something exciting or meaningful within the content. The information should be something that lights a fire in your belly so that you have a visceral need to share what you have learned. The excitement that you are experiencing internally is further deepening your mind's connection to your soul.

However, we can still fall short in the development phase when we focus all of our time crafting what we want to say, searching for the perfect turn of phrase or a fresh idea. But truly effective communication comes from engaging your whole, three-dimensional self—mind, body, and soul. We know the content is crucial, but it's also essential to ask: How can we communicate the content with our bodies and our words? Delivery isn't just about speaking the written material, it also involves how we use the space, how we use breath as an impulse, how we gesture, how we connect with the audience. All of these things will lead you to authentic embodiment of the material to make it your own.

Think about this: how do you prepare for your presentations? Do you run through it in your head at your desk as you are editing? Do you mutter to yourself important points in the car on the way to the venue? These examples may seem like preparation, but they fall short of embodiment.

I recommend rehearsing your material on your feet at least three times before presenting. Embodiment comes through intentional, mindful movement. It is essential to make choices about how and where you move in the presentation space. Without physical practice, you risk falling back on habitual movements, which may not always serve your message. While some habits may work for you, others can detract or distract from what you're trying to communicate.

Dr. Albert Mehrabian was a professor of psychology at University of California, Los Angeles. He is best known for his studies in verbal and nonverbal communication. His studies show that only 7% of communication is the content, the words. 38% is vocal (tone, inflection of the voice) and 55% is visual (body movement). That means 93% of your communication is your voice and body! Isn't that an eye-opening statistic? I hope it will spur you to make shifts in how you prepare your content. It's not just about what you say, it's about how you say it with your entire being.

It's important to be intentional about your movements, just as you are with your words. If you don't make deliberate choices, you'll default to habit. It's also important to remember that every "body" is different. Your life experiences have shaped how your body moves in the world and affects how you carry yourself. Be aware of these influences as you develop your communication style, but don't be tempted to imitate others. You are uniquely you, and no one else has had your experiences. Embrace that individuality.

Your communication practice is a lot like learning to ride a bike. As a child, you practiced over and over until one day, you could ride without assistance. Years later, you can still hop on a bike and ride—it's muscle memory. Or imagine the moment when you enter your house and all the lights are off. Without thinking about it, your body knows where the light switch is, and you have light in the room immediately. But do the same thing the first night in a hotel room, and you'll be patting the wall with your hand for several moments searching for the light switch in complete darkness. Your body remembers your house, but has no practice with the hotel room. Your body won't remember your presentation if you don't put your talk on your feet. If you practice mindful movement, your body will retain that knowledge. When it's time to present, you won't have to think about every gesture; your body will know what to do, allowing you to focus on your message.

Unfortunately, nearly half of the communicators I've worked with do not practice their presentations on their feet before speaking (but they do now!). By not physically preparing, their bodies are unable to put their movement choices into muscle memory. Sometimes the lack of full embodiment can lead to a hyper-focus on the content, creating even more disconnect between the mind and body. The speaker then becomes not much more than a talking head.

This happened to Joe, who was still editing and making changes to his pitch one hour before a crucial sales presentation. He was anxious, feeling the pressure to land this client and meet his company's financial goals. He rewrote his pitch multiple times, but right before the meeting he realized his rewrite didn't align with his visual aids. His nerves distracted him from his real goal: showing the client how the product would be of great benefit to their company. He was so focused on word-smithing his content, he neglected to warm up, practice putting the new content into his body, or grounding himself before presenting. As a result, his presentation fell flat, the client chose another firm, and Joe didn't get the promotion for landing the client.

Joe's situation is a strong reminder of the importance of preparation—not just with the content but also in practicing the talk ahead of time to find connection to the material. It's not enough to focus on the manuscript alone; you need to connect all of you with what you're saying. Only then will you truly be able to communicate with authentic impact.

It would have been best for Joe to trust the content he had already prepared. Even if he felt there were missing pieces. He was focused on making the intellectual material better rather than embodying it. Content creation is so much more than the words we choose—it's the way we choose to embody our words that connects us.

SPECIAL NOTE:

Some speakers don't have the opportunity to create their own content. They may have to present material that has been written for them, and this can pose a challenge if the speaker doesn't feel connected to the content. However, having content created for you is particularly useful when selling a product or explaining a new piece of equipment. The people writing the material for the presentation know the product inside and out, and this pre-written content can save you time and energy. Lean into that gift so you will be able to focus on making sure the delivery is interesting and authentic. The writers have crafted skeletal material, leaving space for you to flesh it out with your own personality. Instead of spending the bulk of your time creating content, you have so much more time to bring elements of you into the presentation. When shaping pre-written content, make it your own by weaving in personal stories, finding appropriate moments of levity, and trusting the writers.

2
You Don't Know What You Don't Know

"Curiosity is one of the permanent and certain characteristics of a vigorous mind."

— Samuel Johnson

In the fall of 1985, when big hair, giant shoulder pads, funky makeup, and neon clothing were dominating the culture, I began my training to become an actor. I couldn't wait to step onto the stage to perform in front of an audience. However, I was blindsided by the amount of rigorous training required to become a serious actor. What I thought would be "big play" demanded a great deal of work and focus. In the first couple of years, the foundation of my acting training was learning the technical and most efficient use of my voice and body. Initially, I was overwhelmed that we had to do so much work to understand breath support for projection and articulation of the voice, freeing our voice from tension, using breath as the impulse for vocal and physical movement, and really working on development of physical and vocal flexibility. I just wanted to perform!

Looking back now, there was so much that I didn't know about acting training, and I now know why technique was such a large focus of my training. The techniques I learned were patterned into my muscle memory, and my body was integrating what I was learning. Having good technique took my focus off the physical and vocal choices I was using for my character, and over time, the technique took care of itself. I was then able to work on other things while developing a three-dimensional character. When acting, your job is to bring a character to life with your entire instrument, mind, body, and soul. The audience shouldn't see the actor working, rather, they should believe that you are the character. My training was about understanding how to use my instrument to support my performance so that the audience only saw the character being, not the actor working.

As I moved from theatre into spaces working with public speakers, I soon realized that most of the speakers I was coaching had given little to no thought to their movement. I could see that they knew their content extremely well (mind), they believed what they were saying (soul), but their voice and movement (body) were not on the same page. They virtually became talking heads, disconnected from their bodies. I assumed that such foundational things would be taught in seminary, business schools, or other training environments for communicators. I was mistaken.

So what happens when a speaker begins their career without that foundational training? Many speakers know that they should pay *some* attention to movement—but it often shows up through applying random positive notes or feedback, which can be overemphasized or misunderstood.

That is exactly what happened to Ryan. He was a pastor with solid content in his message, but his physicality was completely out of sync with his message and quite off-putting. He would move across the stage, take a wide stance with his legs, place his hands on his hips, and thrust his pelvis forward (and I'm not joking). This repeated movement throughout his message was distracting, and it had no connection to the content he was delivering. When I asked him about his habitual movement pattern, he explained that his professor had told him to move around the stage to engage the audience and to take a "power stance" for greater authority. Unfortunately, these well-intended instructions left him disconnected from both his content and himself. What started as helpful advice had turned into a distracting habit that undermined his message. In fact, he had no idea how off-putting it was. No one had ever told him how his "power stance" was distracting his audience away from the very content he was trying to communicate. He simply didn't know what he didn't know.

My curiosity regarding the somatic (mind-body connection) training gap led me to investigate what students of communication, business, marketing, and theology were being taught in higher education. What I found was very surprising. More than 90% of the seminaries I contacted had no dedicated voice or body classes in their curricula. Some offered elective courses in public speaking or body language, but very few focused on helping students discover and develop their authentic voice and physical presence. I also found this to be true of business, marketing and communications programs in several schools. They did not offer vocal and body classes as part of their core training. In higher education, it seems to be about getting all the intellectual information but most of the schools are missing the other two pieces of the trifecta—body and soul.

While I was curiously investigating different programs, I had the opportunity to speak with some of the professors teaching in theology programs at multiple universities.

Several of the professors mentioned students would receive feedback on their voice and movement during a course called homiletics. Homiletics is the art and science of public preaching which includes preparation and delivery of a homily or sermon. I asked many professors how they taught physical and vocal techniques in these Homelitics classes. I discovered the feedback the students were receiving on voice, body and delivery revolved around "what not to do." "Don't pace!" Don't point!" Don't tug on your clothes!" The "don't" notes often leave speakers hyper-focused on what not to do when they are preaching. The end result is ironically that they end up doing the exact thing they were told not to do. "Don't" notes teach them what not to do, instead of training on how to choose what they should do. The speaker ends up unsure of what to do with their voice and body. They end up stuck in their heads, disconnected from their bodies, their message, and their audience. Instead of seeing their personal "isms" as a negative, speakers should learn how to leverage their unique patterns to support their content.

"Ism" is another word that I use interchangeably with habit. Habits are things you do physically without thinking, which can become a distraction if they do not support your message. They show up as nervous energy, tension, and repetitive gestures when communicating. By understanding the significance of movement and breath, communicators can move from unconscious movement patterns ("isms") to purposeful, impactful presentations.

For example, I once worked with a client who constantly put his hands in his pockets. His habit stemmed from a compliment he received from someone remarking that he looked at ease while speaking with his hands in his pockets. Unfortunately, he overused this gesture, constantly putting his hands in his pockets. Because his hands were in his pockets he was unable to gesture with his hands and he started lifting his shoulders up to his ears, creating an unintentional shrug. His physical habit of hand in the pockets with the addition of the shoulder shrug made him appear uncertain about his content and disconnected his body from his message. Imagine trying to be compelling about your topic while your body looks like it doesn't even want to be there.

Some other common habits include lip-smacking, tugging at your clothes, pointing at your audience, pacing or not moving at all, tied too closely to notes, swaying side to side, or gesturing excessively. You probably know the one that rings true for you. Perhaps you've been told "don't" in a feedback session. As you identify your habits, my encouragement to you is to resist the urge to judge them. Simply acknowledge them. That being said, all movements have meaning, so if you're moving without purpose, it distracts from what you're trying to convey. Often, excessive movement comes from uncontained nervousness, manifesting as habitual gestures that don't support your content.

The best starting point for understanding embodied communication is considering why you move the way you do. Habitual gestures and movement patterns are a unique part of your story. Simply start observing yourself throughout your day. Observe your movement patterns without judgment and avoid labeling your habits as good or bad. The goal of getting to know what you do physically when speaking (and in everyday life) is so that you will be able to acknowledge your isms and expand your movement vocabulary beyond your habits to effectively communicate. Start taking notes on how you move every day. Get curious about your own physical body and voice. Here is a cursory list of questions to consider about your movement:

- How do you move?
- How do you sit or stand?
- Where do you hold tension in your body?
- How do you breathe?
- Do you hold your breath? When and where does this happen during your day?

- Do you run out of breath at the end of sentences?
- How do you walk, and at what tempo?
- What's the relationship between your arms and body when walking?
- How do your feet connect with the ground as you walk?
- Do you gesture a lot when you talk, or are you more comfortable in stillness?
- Are your gestures random, or do they support what you're saying?
- Do you speak quickly or slowly?
- Are there physical or vocal fillers you frequently use?
- During conversations, do you look at the person you're speaking with, or do you glance around?
- What's your spatial relationship with others when having a conversation? Are you close to them, mid-range, or far away?
- What does your voice sound like to you?
- How do you move when interacting with people?

Record your observations about your movement in a notebook or a voice memo. If you don't know what your personal movement patterns are, investigate. Knowing yourself is the beginning of authentic communication. Use the observation practice above to discover what your physical neutral is, your blank canvas. Knowing your "neutral" means having an understanding of your habits, and why you might have those particular habits. Having this knowledge about yourself also allows you to let go of things you were told to do that are not authentic to you. Release all borrowed gestures that you have picked up from other speakers and step into who you are, not who you were told to be.

A few years ago, I met a woman named Julie at a speaking conference. She co-wrote a bestselling book that launched her into the speaking circuit, but she confided in me that she felt out of her depth on stage. Her co-writer/co-presenter was highly energetic, gregarious, took up lots of space, and was quite loud when they were on stage together. Julie was often given feedback that she needed to be louder, move more, and match his energy. But applying those notes made her feel uncomfortable in her own skin. We agreed to work together with some very specific speaking goals in mind. The first time I observed her presentation, I noticed she would hold her hands in front of her body—a protective gesture—and often ran out of breath near the end of her sentences. Her nerves were affecting her ability to take full, deep breaths and resulted in shallow breathing. She was "running out of gas" at the end of most of her phrases.

Through our working sessions, we discovered that her personal movement preferences were completely at odds with the feedback she had received. She felt very uncomfortable trying to match the energy of her speaking counterpart because that was not who she was authentically. Once she knew and understood her movement preferences, she was able to start making choices mindfully about how she wanted to move in the spaces where she was communicating. We worked on expanding her physical vocabulary and breath capacity. She learned to embrace her own style. By staying true to herself, Julie gained confidence and began to embody her content authentically. She was empowered!

An important takeaway from Julie's story is that everyone has different preferences for movement and communication. Variety is the spice of life! If both speakers in a duo like Julie and her co-author exhibit similar high energy, the audience could become weary, especially if one of those speakers is pushing for effect. With the awareness of her movement preferences, Julie locked into a grounded, calm presence, which complemented her co-author's energetic style. They were then able to connect with a wider audience because they were both being themselves.

As you think about strengthening your communications game, focus on developing a practice that is authentic and resonates with you. Continue learning how you use your voice and body in everyday life and when communicating. Identify and acknowledge your physical habits, even if you're unsure of where they stem from. Once you know what your habits are, practice by allowing yourself to use them 3 times in your message. You will be honoring your history but also looking for some new physical and vocal choices to fill the gaps. Here's a trick if you are still unsure of what your habits may be: film yourself when presenting and then scrub through the video at high speed. Using this method will reveal patterns/habits that you may not have noticed before. One of my former clients would have benefited from this practice.

Brian had a habit of tugging the front of his shirt down while speaking. After one of his talks, I noted that he had pulled on his shirt 168 times. He had no idea it had become such a distracting habit, so distracting, that it caused the listener to stop listening. When I asked him where he thought pulling on the front of his shirt may have come from, I saw a lightbulb go on. He had recently lost 75 pounds, and pulling on the front of his shirt was something he would do habitually to make sure his stomach wasn't showing. He had no awareness that he was still doing it. His speech was filled with other small, habitual gestures—many of which he had picked up from speakers he admired. These movements weren't his own, and before we could improve his communication style, we had to strip away those habits and get to the core of who he was as a speaker.

Discovering your authentic self in voice and body requires intentional practice. Make choices about how you use the space, where you move, and how you gesture. Think about the story that your body is telling, as well as the words you are saying. It takes time, but it will bring the content you are creating to a new level. Mindful movement would be a great tool to add to your communications practice.

We should all be lifelong learners, and the desire to

improve your craft will require being open to new systems, new strategies, and new experiences. Every experience provides learning opportunities. Some approaches will feel natural, while others may challenge you or even feel uncomfortable. Embrace this discomfort and be curious about why certain methods don't resonate with you. Ask questions, try new techniques, and continuously refine your approach. Sometimes you'll find that the refining requires more introspection and consideration; always being mindful of your authentic self in the process.

The more curious you are about yourself—your voice, your body, and your movement—the stronger a communicator you'll become. So, embrace the unknown, what you don't know, and keep learning who you are. You'll be amazed at how much there is to discover about you, your body, your habits, and how embodied movement will allow your content to have greater impact. Discovering your authentic voice and body requires mindful, intentional movement work. It takes time, but it will bring the content you are delivering to a new level of excellence.

3
All Movement Has Meaning

"What you do speaks so loud that I cannot hear what you say."
— *Ralph Waldo Emerson*

Have you heard the old saying, "Actions speak louder than words?" The quote usually refers to a person's character, but I think it is a phrase that communicators should ponder in a different context. Have you ever watched a communicator and found yourself so distracted by their "actions" (a physical or vocal habit), that you stop listening to their talk? The physical and vocal habits we fall into while speaking can become "automatic pilot" fillers that can prevent your content from landing with your audience. When I notice a speaker's habits, I will sometimes start counting how many times they occur instead of focusing on their presentation. If I'm doing this, your audience might be too, and that is a problem.

Paul's "actions" spoke louder than his words in a message I observed. Paul was a pastor that had the unconscious habit of lip-smacking when he was communicating. Initially, I thought his mouth was dry and he needed a drink of water, but after a few minutes, it became clear this was an ingrained habit. By the end of his twenty-minute talk, I had counted over 180 lip-smacks, and I couldn't really tell you what his message was about. After some post-message conversation and investigation, it turned out that his lip smacking habit was linked to extreme jaw tension. It's not possible to simply wish habits away; you need to actively work to change them through physical practice and exercises. For Paul, we worked on some jaw releasing exercises, added shoulder mobility work to free him from tension, and began implementing vocal warm-ups to begin his journey towards minimizing his habit. Without making mindful movement choices, practicing movement on your feet, your unconscious habits will show up every time you communicate.

What we say has meaning, we can all agree—the words we choose mean things, and we work very hard as communicators to select the best possible words when we speak. But somehow, we don't address the role our bodies play when we are communicating those words. And that is a mistake. Movement during presentations holds as much significance as the content itself (93% to be exact). It's one thing to eliminate "meaningless" movement (the unconscious habits), but it's another thing altogether to find meaning in our movement. We need to add mindfulness into our preparation process for movement so that the movement is aligned with what we are communicating. If we don't consciously choose how, where, and when we move during a talk, we will miss the opportunity to fully embody our message. Just like words, all movement has meaning, and whether it is intentional, habitual, or subconscious, that movement will communicate *something*. As a speaker, you should be choosing what your movement is communicating. I know at some level we have all witnessed speakers' unconscious habits getting in the way of their presentations. But we haven't learned the lesson with movement that we understand to be true when it comes to words.

For many speakers, prep focus stays primarily intellectual, making sure the content is logical, helpful, and grounded in truth. But without being mindful of your movement, why bother presenting the material in the first place? Wouldn't it be easier to hand your audience your manuscript and call it a day? You could give them a one-dimensional view of your intellectual content on a piece of paper. But we know why that is insufficient. When speaking, you are a three-dimensional human being on a platform, not just a one-dimensional piece of paper with words. So we must be mindful of our entire selves — mind, body (which includes voice), and soul — while preparing our presentations. It makes sense to start considering how to take your internal intellectual content and move it into external space with your voice and body. Every speaker will do this differently because we have all lived different unique lives. Your specific experiences and physical presence add depth, dimension and texture to your content. So, how can you move your content from one-dimensional text to three-dimensional delivery? By practicing your "blocking!"

Blocking is acting terminology for a character's physical movement in a play from beginning to end. It can also be called a physical score of action because the movement, spatial relationships, shaping, and gestures of the character tell as much of a story as the actual words of the script. The blocking becomes the skeletal structure of the character and the words and emotions become the flesh and bones, so that when the character speaks their lines and moves through the space the character becomes three-dimensional. Through the magic of theatre, the actor transforms a one-dimensional script of words into the three-dimensional embodied character we see in the performance.

I urge all communicators to write their blocking, or physical score of action, on their manuscript. Most speakers already codify their text with reminders regarding other things they think are important in their presentations. Self-coaching notes like "speed up here" or "pause here" are commonly used. All we are doing now is adding some intentional plans for movement to those notes. Come up with a simple code for your manuscript that cues when, where, and how to move during your talk. Once your movement coding is complete, practice your talk on your feet. Yes, on your feet. Remember, we want to allow our muscle memory to take over. When communicating, you should not be thinking about your movement. But if you practice your talk enough times before presenting, your muscle memory will support your choices, allowing the majority of your mindful movement from practice to transfer into your talk. The more you practice your presentations, the more responsive your body will be in holding your choices from rehearsal. The more you work at something, the more proficient you become at that "thing."

When we connect our words to our physicality, that is mindful movement. By connecting the mind, body, and soul we amplify the impact of our message. Using the whole trifecta, we are able to embody the content three-dimensionally. We begin on the page — the one-dimensional connection of the mind. When we add emotional (the soul) connection to the text, we have two dimensions. But to get to three, we must add the movement of our physical body and our vocal cords. Three-dimensional communication will be more impactful in any setting, whether in person, captured on video, or even in virtual meetings.

The more connected you are to your material, the more effective your delivery will be. Every time you communicate, you have the potential to inspire someone, motivating them to shift their thinking or move them in a new direction. Speaking requires more than just good content—it requires content that is developed, delivered, and refined within a framework of continuous improvement. When we focus on content and delivery, we can create powerful moments for our audience. But this takes practice. You need to know your material inside and out, make mindful movement choices, practice your content on your feet, connect with your breath, and be willing to leave old physical habits behind that no longer serve you as a speaker.

So, what are the new practices you are considering implementing in light of this revelation? How will you begin to implement a physical score of action, how can you address the unconscious habits you have formed in your presentations? Remember, all movement has meaning, so use that intentional movement to support your content. Don't leave it to chance. Choosing your movement is just as important as choosing your words. I can't wait for you to experience how mindful movement will bring your speaking game to the next level. Movement is powerful and it is a game changer!

4
Claiming Your Space

"I taught myself to be as fluent as possible in nonverbal languages because it's the only way to understand what people aren't saying, to carve out your space and claim it. It's the only way

I can feel like I know what's going on."

— *Marieke Nijkamp, Even If We Break*

Mike stepped onto the platform with his head hanging forward, chin close to his chest, shoulders rounded forward, arms hanging down close to the sides of his body. The steps that he took were very short; heel to toe with not much of a stride. As he began to speak, his voice was very soft, light, with not much vocal variety. He lifted his head a few inches to look at his audience and raised his eyebrows, causing tension in his forehead. He proceeded to stand behind the podium for his entire message. He didn't use the platform space at all, staying behind his notes most of the time — but not using them. The content was interesting but his delivery fell flat. I knew Mike personally, but I didn't know the Mike I was seeing at that moment.

Mike was a 6'5" man with an enormous wingspan, a great laugh, and a strong connected speaking voice. When he was finished communicating, I shared my observations with him, mentioning that I felt he was making himself smaller and not effectively claiming his space. As I explained my observations of seeing him narrow in the space, it was almost as if he wanted to disappear. His eyes got wide and he said, "I know what is happening!" He shared that he worries about his height being distracting — he didn't want to scare his audience with big moves or sudden gestures. He chose to stay as still as possible so people could reflect on what he was saying. He also thought that this communicated a certain kind of humility. In actuality, his body wasn't connected which caused the listener to disconnect from Mike as the speaker. It was a breakthrough in his work as a speaker to be free from these misguided assumptions. He was now opened to a new world of connected movement possibilities, paving the way for him to claim the space with his whole self. We worked on gestures that would take his arms away from his body, looked for places to speed up to increase the urgency in his talk, and practiced stepping away from his notes (which he wasn't referencing anyway), using unexplored areas of the stage. I created unique exercises for him to connect his mind, body, and soul. The exercises brought him back to an authentic place by stripping away his facade of humility. It was exciting to watch the transformation as he became Mike, the guy I knew!

Mike isn't the only communicator I have worked with who struggled to use their platform space confidently. Claiming your space will look different for everyone. Begin the process of using your space by authentically walking onto the platform, being comfortable in your own skin without pushing for effect. It would be beneficial for speakers to intentionally use their space to support their content in a way that is comfortable for them. If communicators have considered movement or use of space at all, it is often on a very basic level, but that's actually a good place to start. When thinking about using your platform, explore the room, considering the "why" behind your physical choices.

The benefits of confidently moving around the stage are numerous: the movement provides visual variety, can support your words, and reads as a comfortability in your own skin. When you move with intention, your gestures and position on the platform can enhance your connection with the audience. That being said, overdoing it can make you seem pushy or ungrounded, so authenticity is key. The goal is to strike a balance between activity and stillness, existing in the space in a way that feels authentic and intentional to you.

Susan struggled with imposter syndrome. As soon as she stepped onto the stage, she instinctively clasped her hand in front of her torso, bent her knees, and raised her shoulders in a shrug with a side tilt to her head. The way she stood on stage communicated, "I shouldn't be here," "I'm sorry to bother you," "I really don't know much," "Don't get mad at me for being here." Her body narrowed in the space, and when she bent her knees she would sink down towards the ground. The way she moved in the space seemed like a subconscious physical apology for being in the room.

When I shared my observations with her, she was surprised her body was conveying that information in the space. Susan explained that she was one of the first women to speak at her church. She was feeling the weight of making a way for other female speakers that would come behind her. Susan was also worried about the response of the congregation, as she didn't want to offend anyone. She had spent hours preparing her manuscript, but hadn't thought about practicing her content while on her feet, nor did she consider how to prepare her voice and body. Like many speakers, she focused solely on content and overlooked the importance of voice, body, or use of space.

Most of the time we are on autopilot when it comes to movement, unaware of the signals our body and voice send when we are communicating. We don't think about movement most of the time. For example, if we are thirsty we get up for a glass of water. If we are tired we sit down. If we see something on the floor in front of us, we instinctively step over the object or pick it up. However, speakers must make intentional choices about how to use the space to support their content. If you don't prepare your body, your subconscious habits will show up every time. As human beings, our body and voice are our instruments. If we aren't mindful of our whole self we risk tripping over our words, falling into unintentional physical patterns, which will diminish the impact of our carefully crafted content.

Susan, like Mike, did not claim her space. Conversely,

we have met people who take up too much space. There are doctors, lawyers, and many other professions where people over inhabit the spaces where they work. They are pushing or trying to project confidence and knowledge to their patients/clients. It is almost as if they are trying to convince themselves of the next best step with their words. When these folks are not connected, this can come across to patients as ego or indifference. How we enter and inhabit space—physically and vocally—profoundly affects the people in the room. Claiming your space isn't about pretending to be something you're not; it's about becoming more fully who you are in that moment. Finding the balance between confidence and humility is important for every communicator.

A very important part of a communicator's process is in the preparation it takes to step onto the platform and authentically take up space in the room. It takes work to acknowledge habits, strip away the years of facade, work towards authenticity, to claim your space. Something that will help you when communicating is to have an understanding of how to intentionally use the stage to connect with your audience.

Take a look at the stage spaces of a traditional proscenium stage on the diagram below. These are areas of the stage that theatre directors mindfully use to help them tell the playwright's story. These same stage spaces could also be used by communicators to support their content. A speaker can choose different areas of the platform to connect with the audience in an intentional way. Think about how you might be able to map your movement on your manuscript so you can begin to deliver your content using the space more effectively.

Upstage Right (or Up Right)	Upstage	Upstage Left (or Up Left)
Stage Right	Center Stage	Stage Left
Downstage Right (or Down Right)	Downstage	Downstage Left (or Down Left)

AUDIENCE

- **Downstage Center:** When moving to this area, you are closing a gap between you and your listeners by getting closer to them without anything between you. You can use this space when telling a personal story, moving away from your podium to tell a story you know by heart. The spatial relationship with you and your audience will allow an opportunity for them to be drawn into the story.
- **Stage Right:** Talk about good/positive things on stage right. Move down right, to be closer to your audience or use the space upstage right which puts some distance between you and them, keeping them at arm's length. Western audiences read from left to right as they are looking at you, so this part of the stage holds more focus naturally.
- **Stage Left:** When talking about bad/negative things use stage left. If you move downstage left there is an element of closing the spatial gap. Moving upstage left gives them a bit of room to breathe.
- **Up Stage:** You are putting more distance between you and your listeners.
- **Center Stage:** A grounded, powerful space, that can be used for direct communication or key moments.

Practice your movement in combination with deciding in advance how to use your space and you will connect with your audience in a more authentic way. Just remember that too much movement can become distracting, so balance your use of space with intention. Find moments of stillness during important moments in your talk. Know when to pause, stand still, slow down, and let your message sink in without excessive movement. Plan these moments—they might not come naturally without connecting them to intention.

Another trap can be repetitive content; auto-pilot can kick in when you give the same talk over and over. The speaker may begin rushing, causing the content to sound glib. Repetition of specific gestures, standing position, and emphasizing words for dramatic effect repetitively can create an inauthentic slickness. Continue to look for ways to keep your content fresh so that when you present the material it is as if you are speaking about it for the first time.

As you begin to consider using different parts of the space for your message the process of claiming your space has begun! Keep being curious as you play with different spaces of the stage. Your use of space will support your content as you speak and move.

Side note: If you are hired to speak in a new space, a place you have never been before, ask questions about the environment before you arrive. Learn everything you can about the space and equipment they use. You could ask for them to send a wide shot of the space so you have a sense of how big the room is and where the people will be sitting. Understanding the layout helps you rehearse so when you are communicating in the room you use the space more effectively. Seeing the room will also help you "fill the space" and connect with everyone present. A speaker who is comfortable in the room will naturally claim it, allowing the audience to settle in and really listen to the presentation.

Using the information given to you about the room where you will be presenting, set up a rehearsal space for yourself. Now you are able to begin making mindful choices about your movement on your feet. Once your space is prepared, videotape the initial reading of your manuscript on your "set". I talk about video capture as a tool often in this book as it can be extremely helpful. The practice of recording the first read of your talk on your feet is different from videotaping your full presentations. When watching the video of your first read through, you will see your initial instincts for movement and gesture. For the camera set-up on this recording, make sure you can see your whole body in the frame. Give yourself plenty of room in your recording space to move front to back and side to side. Place your notes on a separate table so you aren't holding them for this taping. The goal is to notice impulses in your body. For example, you might see yourself start to move stage right but then hesitate. You might notice wrist movement, shifting your palm ever so slightly forward. These impulses might lead to intentional decisions about following through with gesture and movement in your full presentation. Pay attention to where these impulses show up on your video, and make note of them on your manuscript for rehearsal. This practice sets the table for you to make choices about how to use and claim your space authentically, while identifying the gestures that support your content. Ultimately, claiming your space is about embracing your unique movement style, being present with the people you are communicating with, and filling the space without pushing for effect.

5
If You Aren't Connected You Won't Connect

"The body never lies."

– Martha Graham

Over the years of teaching college students, I noticed they were struggling to embody their characters, focusing more on the emotional connection, memorization of text, and their final performances. They had intellectual knowledge about the character they were playing, but did not have "body knowledge" of how the characters showed up physically in their performances.

It puzzled me how difficult it was (and sometimes impossible) for students to implement adjustments on the physical life of their characters. They would make a few physical changes, however those temporary adjustments only looked as if the actor was "working hard" to do it. At the end of the day, they were unable to hold or embody the changes. It was only a matter of time before they reverted back to their own habits/isms.

Similarly, I was seeing the same disembodied phenomenon happening with the speakers I was coaching. These communicators didn't consider how their bodies could support the content they were delivering. And, just like the acting students, I was unable to connect to the speakers because they weren't embodied, they were disconnected. It was clear to me that the problem was one and the same for both groups. They were stuck in their own personal patterns. Their physical habits would keep showing up until they made a very intentional shift in their movement preparation.

While reflecting on how to help these speakers connect with their audiences, I was studying Laban Movement Analysis, a somatic practice that connects mind and body. As I worked through Irmgard Bartenieff's Six Fundamentals (thigh lift, lateral pelvic shift, forward pelvic shift, body half, knee drop, and arm circles), I experienced a stripping away, a release for myself that was so profound I noted this experience. I wondered if this neutralizing, or coming back to oneself, could be possible for others who struggled similarly.

While we were studying Bartenieff's Six Fundamentals we also learned about Peggy Hackney. In her book, *Making Connections: Total Body Integration Through Bartenieff Fundamentals*, she discusses developmental patterns from birth to age five. In order, the Patterns of Connectivity are 1) breath 2) core - distal connectivity 3) head - tail connectivity 4) upper-lower connectivity 5) body-half connectivity and 6) cross-lateral connectivity. Most children move through all of these developmental patterns, unless there is a disruption in development. As babies and toddlers explore the world with their voices and bodies, they pass through these six stages. Some children may skip one or more of these patterns or not move through all of them fully. The lack of these patterns during development can be moved through as adults when recognized and treated intentionally.

Over the last several years, I have found the Patterns of Connectivity to be a great tool that assists communicators to "neutralize" their physical habits. Finding a neutral place from which to start helps speakers connect more fully with their audience by being present in their own bodies. When I teach my clients the Patterns of Connectivity, I call it "re-patterning." This work allows them to let go of the facade, neutralize habits, and remember who they were created to be before life happened to them.

Practicing these patterns in developmental order for an extended period of time allows you to begin your journey toward authentic mindful movement —movement that can only be attributed to you. I have witnessed this not only with my clients but also in my own life. I have found that working through these patterns each day reminds the body of how to go back to childhood, and find the fun in work, while at the same time letting go of habits that are blocking connection to audiences. Practicing the Patterns of Connectivity has the possibility to remind us who we were created to be and allows us to step into who we are today.

Below you will find a very cursory explanation of Peggy Hackney's Patterns of Connectivity, in order to give you a taste of how you might see them in childhood development.

Breath: The very first thing that a baby does when they are born is take their first three-dimensional breath and sometimes when they exhale, they let out a good cry. If a baby is born vaginally, the baby will twist out of their mother's body, imprinting the spiraling or diagonal (the diagonal goes from a shoulder to the opposite hip) in their body that will eventually be used in cross lateral work a few years down the road.

Core-Distal Connectivity: Core is at the naval center of your body and the distal points are the furthest "distance" away from your core: fingertips, the top of your head, between your legs, and your toes. Imagine a baby on their back in a crib with hanging toys above them. They kick at them and bat at them with their hands and feet. They are constantly putting things into their mouth (including their toes) as they explore the world around them. They are reaching out into the world with their distal points and bringing things into their mouth or closer to their core to see, discover, and learn about their environment.

Head-Tail Connectivity: There is a constant conversation going on between a baby's head and tail. Lots of counter balancing with this pattern, children are beginning to learn how their spine will support them. The use of tummy time for babies, helps them strengthen their necks. If they are on their belly, they will lift their head to see the things around them and eventually they will push up with their hands and arms to see more of the room. They then will drop their head and push their bottom up in the air, while their face is on the blanket. Back and forth they go, head up and bottom down, bottom up and head down. Eventually their neck becomes strong enough so they can use their spine to support them as they roll over, sit up, stand, crawl, and eventually walk.

Upper-Lower Connectivity: After experiencing their spine on the floor, babies begin scooting on the floor. With this pattern, they stabilize their "lower" body and pull themselves forward with their hands; they then stabilize their "upper" body and mobilize while their lower body pushes them forward. They are using their arms and legs to push and pull them when they scoot and crawl on the floor. Eventually they pull themselves up to standing at the coffee table or sofa and hold steady with their hands. They walk a little way with their feet, and their lower half stays still until their arms and hands catch up with their feet. They are cruising the furniture in upper/lower.

Body-Half Connectivity: Now things are getting fun! Imagine there is a vertical line down your body dividing your left side from your right side. The next thing that happens developmentally is the baby lets go of the coffee table and walks forward like a little baby zombie; first the right side moves, then the left side moves, and so it goes until they are more confident on their feet and they move into the final pattern of connectivity.

Cross-Lateral Connectivity: Here the child begins walking but no longer in body half - no longer "left side, then right side." They are moving in cross lateral, meaning that their arms are moving in opposition to their legs. They have found the diagonal in their body.

What I have explained above is a very basic overview, but what I experienced with the Patterns of Connectivity was freeing. This freedom led to a releasing of habits and an overall sense of "letting go." I discovered that mindfully going through the Patterns of Connectivity in developmental order allows you to be more fully connected, it brings you back to yourself, and allows you to authentically connect with others more effectively.

I saw this process play out with my students as they were able to better understand who they were authentically in voice and body before trying to embody a character. The Patterns of Connectivity also helped my speaker clients let go of the masks they put on in different environments. Observing them practicing the patterns allowed them to strip away the masks and rediscover their authenticity, grounding them in who they were created to be in voice and body.

I even had the experience using the Patterns of Connectivity closer to home. While I was learning about Hackney's work, my eleven-year-old daughter was a member of a competitive dance team. Around this time most of the girls in her age group were learning pirouettes, fouettés, and turn sequences. My kiddo was struggling, falling out of her turns, losing her center. Then, all of a sudden, it dawned on me! She was born via cesarean section and never experienced the first spiraling motion during birth, which would have imprinted the diagonal in her body. As I reflected back on her physical development as a child, I realized she had not moved through all of the patterns of connectivity. She hadn't fully crawled as a baby; she would walk forward with her hands, wheel with her right leg, foot on the floor and crawl on her left knee. So her diagonal and cross-lateral patterns weren't fully developed. This revealed even more of a reason that she was not finding the diagonal when turning. We spent a couple of weeks working through the patterns of connectivity in order: breath, core-distal, head-tail, upper-lower, body-half, and cross-lateral. Sometimes we would work through the patterns laying on the floor or sometimes we would do a sequence while standing. My goal was to help her to find the diagonal in her body that didn't happen naturally. To find it we would work to connect the right shoulder to the left hip or the left arm diagonally through the body to the right leg. Eventually, she was able to turn successfully as her body was able to remember how to use the diagonal.

Throughout our lifetime, our developmental patterns are disrupted, causing our bodies to overcompensate for what has happened to us, and that is when physical habits are formed. Years ago, I had a student who experienced extreme trauma and whenever she tried to share something personal, she took on a posture that was the opposite of open. She was saying she was being open and vulnerable, but her body was saying something entirely different. She was closing herself off physically, seemingly to protect herself. She would enclose, sink, then retreat with the lower half of her body, while crossing her legs and arms in front of her torso. She had been through something profound in her life that caused her to move into a physical positioning of self-protection when speaking vulnerably about herself.

Habits like these, whether they involve posture or movement, don't always serve the message we're trying to convey. When they present as habits, they can distract from the content. But when we align effective movement with our words, we create a more impactful message. Since the goal is to connect with our audiences, we can easily understand there will be difficulty if we ourselves are not connected to our breath and bodies. Once you have uncovered patterns that aren't fully expressed, we work to pinpoint how that shows up in physical habits, acknowledge them, and re-pattern to release them. There are additional exercises available for re-patterning that I use with my clients 1:1 to neutralize these tendencies.

The closer you are to full connection in mind, body, and soul (*The Speaker's Trifecta*), the more effective you will be in extending that connection to your audience. The exploratory work that comes through the Six Fundamentals and the Patterns of Connectivity is the path toward full body exploration and re-patterning. Neglecting this part of the process is a recipe for disaster — and will lead to a further separation between the speaker and the audience. The audience may not be able to identify why they are not connecting, but they will not connect all the same. It's your job to do the work to explore not just what an embodied speaker looks like, but specifically and uniquely what you need to do to be fully embodied and connected.

6
Breath as Impulse

"Breath is the bridge which connects life to consciousness, which unites your body to your thoughts. Whenever your mind becomes scattered, use your breath as the means to take hold of your mind again."

— *Thich Nhat Hanh, The Miracle of Mindfulness: An Introduction to the Practice of Meditation*

Most of our bodily systems are working on their own without much opportunity for us to have an impact on them with our mind. When most body systems are failing, or giving us trouble, we can't redirect simply by thinking about how to make them work properly. However, we can use our mind to slow down or speed up our breathing, take deep breaths, or take shallow breaths because of our mind-body connection. Breathing is something we do automatically. We don't give much thought to how we breathe until someone brings it to our attention. For the most part, breathing goes like this: when you breathe, you inhale oxygen into your lungs, which expand as your diaphragm moves downward. At the top of your inhale, when your lungs are full, there's a natural impulse to exhale. As you exhale, the diaphragm moves upward, and carbon dioxide is released either through your nose, mouth, or both. At the bottom of the exhale, when no more air is left in your body, you'll notice the impulse to inhale again. Breath is life giving.

Here's an exercise you can try to mindfully connect to your breath. Sit comfortably in a chair with both feet flat on the floor with hands resting on your knees. Close your eyes and notice your breath. What happens to your body when you inhale, or when you exhale? Do you breathe through your nose, your mouth, or both? What is the temperature of the air as it enters your body? Is the carbon dioxide leaving your body the same temperature as the oxygen that entered your lungs? If you are noticing any tension in your body, there are a few ways to release tension with breath. On the exhale, you can send the breath to the areas of tension in your body, allowing the breath to act as a form of massage. Or you could increase the tension in those muscles on an inhale, hold your breath and very quickly exhale, and release those muscles simultaneously. Finally, you could combine deep breathing and use your hands to massage the tension area until those muscles release.

Now that we are free from tension, let's claim our space by practicing the three-dimensional breath. It moves in three dimensions: top to bottom (vertical), side to side (horizontal), and front to back (sagittal). The three-dimensional breath is happening inside of you, and it causes your torso to take up more space externally, shaping how you move in the world. You can practice this full life-giving breath while sitting, standing, or laying on the floor. For our purposes we will connect to the three-dimensional breath while sitting:

- Move to the edge of the chair.
- Plant both feet flat on the floor.
- Sit up straight, head floating up off the top of your spine.
- Chin should be parallel to the floor.
- Rest your hands on your thighs either palm up or down.
- Release any tension you might have anywhere in your body.
- Breathe, inhale, and exhale at your own pace and focus on your breath.
- Notice at the top of the inhale an impulse to exhale, and conversely at the bottom of the exhale, an impulse to inhale. Try to keep the flow moving without holding your breath.
- Imagine a vertical line running from the top of your head down through your spine in the center of your body, and out down through the seat of the chair. This is your vertical axis, representing a top-to-bottom breath. As you inhale, notice a lengthening of your spine top to bottom on the inhale, and a coming back to neutral on the exhale. Inhale and exhale a few times focusing on the vertical breath. Keep your shoulders still and relaxed. They shouldn't rise up to your ears as you inhale.

The vertical breath is our connection to God or higher power.

- Next, visualize a horizontal line at your waist, running from your right to left side through the center of your body. This is your side-to-side breath. Place your hands on the sides of your body. As you inhale you will feel the widening side to side as your ribs and intercostal muscles expand to make room for the side-to-side breath. On the exhale, your body will come back to center. Breathe in the horizontal dimension a few times, in and out. On the inhale send the energy out, and on the exhale settle back to neutral. The horizontal breath is the connection to the people closest to you—friends, family, and the people you do life with.

- Finally, picture a front to back line extending forward from your navel out through your lower back. This is your sagittal breath. If helpful, put one hand on your abdomen and one hand on your lower back. When you inhale, think of sending your hands and energy forward and back simultaneously. On the exhale your hands will come back to where they started. Breathe a few times focusing on the sagittal breath. The sagittal breath is your connection to the world; it is a going out and making a difference in the world around you. Together, these three lines form the structure of the three-dimensional breath. Now let's put them all together. I would invite you to close your eyes or soften your gaze so that you can focus inward on the three-dimensional breath. Imagine that you are a big balloon. As you inhale, imagine someone blowing you up like a balloon through your mouth. Notice the expanding top to bottom, side to side, and front to back. On the exhale, the person releases the mouth of the balloon as you come back to center. Focus on taking full breaths, making sure you aren't holding your breath on the inhale or the exhale.

Most people think of inhaling as drawing breath inward, but for efficient movement, consider sending energy outward on both the inhale and on the exhale as you are speaking your content. This shift in thinking allows you to be fully present, sending your energy out when you inhale and sending the words into the space when you are communicating. As a speaker, this concept of sending energy out continuously—whether inhaling or exhaling—creates a flow that supports your communication, making it more dynamic, connected, and present.

The three-dimensional breath happens inside your body as does the content in your mind that you are getting ready to communicate; however, when communicating, our job is to bring the internal space (the intellectual content and three-dimensional breath) into the external space outside of you (your voice and body). As we move from internal to external, we need to be mindful of our breath support because it affects our vocal projection, articulation, and physical shaping. Think of physical shaping as how the breath helps the speaker to move physically in the room. Let's go back to the three-dimensional breath for a moment, imagining we are bringing it to the outside of our body. For example, in the vertical breath—the top to bottom breath—there are two different shaping qualities: **rising** and **sinking**. Go ahead and try these shaping qualities and say them as you embody them. Rise through the top of your head and sink down as if someone is pulling you by your tailbone. Go ahead and say the words "rising" and "sinking" as you shape those qualities physically. Next is the horizontal breath—the side-to-side breath—this shaping is **widening** and **enclosing**. When widening, take up space side to side including your arms and legs and say, "widening." When enclosing, cross the midline of your body with your upper and lower body. Do that a few times in different ways, saying "widening" and "enclosing" as you embody the shaping qualities. Finally, we have the sagittal breath—the front to back breath—the shaping that lives in this dimension is **advancing** and **retreating**. These shaping qualities are particularly fun because you can advance and retreat with different parts of your body. For example, advancing (take a few steps forward) with your nose, your feet, your hands, your chest. Go ahead and try those with your body. Next try retreating (take a few steps backwards), leading with the back of your head, your tailbone, or your heels. They all feel very different. There are so many combinations of shaping qualities that you could use to support what you are communicating.

As you embody these shaping qualities, don't forget to play! Have fun finding new and interesting combinations of these shaping elements that will be helpful as you work towards embodying your content. Try some of these on, you might sink and enclose, or rise, enclose, and advance, or retreat and widen. One of my favorite combinations is to widen and rise. Each combination reveals something about your internal state and the content you are communicating to the room, so be intentional about your external shaping. This is where speakers often lose their connection with their audience because they are saying one thing with their words while communicating something entirely different with their bodies. Mindful shaping ensures your body and message align.

It isn't just your physical shaping that needs to be considered, it is also essential to prepare our voice. As speakers our bodies are our instruments, they need to be warmed up and considered as much as everything else. The voice is part of the body. Think of yourself as a "communication athlete," and warm up like one. Just as a runner stretches before a race, a ballet dancer works at the barre before a big performance, or a concert pianist practices scales on a piano before playing an Sonata at Carnegie Hall. There is a huge difference between a voice that is warmed up and one that is not. When it comes to your voice, you should sound the same when communicating as you do in everyday life. In other words, avoid "putting on" an authoritative speaking voice. Be you and use YOUR voice! Below you will find a couple of very practical ways for you to prepare your voice before you communicate.

Vocal Warm-up:

- Stand with four-five inches between the balls of your feet.
- Your chin to be parallel to the floor, head floating up off the top of your spine.
- Allow your arms to hang at your sides.
- With your lips closed, chew and hum.
- Keeping your lips closed, move your tongue around inside of your mouth which will push your cheeks and lips forward. Keep humming.
- Bend your arms at your elbows, bringing your hands up near the sides of your face. Open your eyes, mouth, and hands wide and say, "AH." Tighten your hands into fists, squeeze your eyes tightly closed, squish your lips together as you say, "Ooh."
- Repeat opening and closing several times and don't forget to vocalize.
- With your mouth open, stick your tongue out and down.
- Move the tip of your tongue up towards your nose.
- Move your tongue to the right, to the left, and then in a figure eight a couple of times.
- Place the tip of the tongue behind your lower teeth and stretch the back of your tongue out of your mouth.

- Blow through your lips making the sound of a motorboat. Shake out your face.
- Finally, it's time to get your articulators—lips, teeth, tongue, hard and soft palates—ready. Choose a few tongue twisters and experiment with vocal range, moving from high to low. Some favorites include "Peter Piper," "Suzie Sells Seashells," and repeating "Toy Boat" rapidly.

After your vocal warm-up, continue to stretch out and wake up your whole body. Experiment with the warm-up below but feel free to make adjustments that work for you and your body. Work on the areas of your body where you know you are tense and add as many stretches as you need to feel awake, present, and free from that tension. We will start in the same physical position as we did with the vocal warm-up.

Physical Warm-up:

- Stand with four-five inches between the balls of your feet.
- Hold your chin parallel to the floor with your head floating up off the top of your spine.
- Allow your arms to come to your sides.
- Pull your shoulders up to your ears, release.
- Push your shoulders down, release.
- Push your shoulders forward, release.

- Pull your shoulders back, release.
- Circle your shoulders back in a circle and then forward in a circle.
- Take your right arm out straight in front of you and pull it across your body with your left arm, stretching out the right tricep.
- Take the right arm and put it behind your head with a bent elbow and push down on your right elbow with your left hand as you lean over to the left. This will stretch out your right-side body.
- Repeat the same stretch on the left.
- Lunge forward with your right leg—your right knee should be bent (don't allow your right knee to go past your right toes). Your left leg should be straight behind you. Try to get your left heel as close the floor as possible. Toes on both feet should be pointing forward. You will feel a stretch in your left hip flexor and in your left hamstring.
- Repeat the same stretch on the left side
- Stand on your left leg holding onto a wall or a chair. Bend your right knee bringing the right heel to your seat. You will feel a nice stretch in the front of your right thigh.
- Repeat and do the same on the left side.

Every-"BODY" is different so if you have any other areas in your body that still need to be stretched out, please do so now.

- Shake out your whole body, arms, legs, head, torso.
- Take the flat palms of your hands and pat your face, your head, and say, "Ah" as you work down the front of your body patting with an open hand. With medium pressure pat your chest, abdomen, front of your thighs, calves, and all the way down the front of your body. Pat out the back side of your body as you reverse the order. Pat the back of your calves, your thighs, your seat, your lower back, your arms, and then just shake everything out as you continue to vocalize. This exercise wakes up your voice, will help release any tension you might be holding, and it will get your blood flowing.

After warming up, reconnect with your three-dimensional breath. The breath is your opportunity to ground yourself, and this process will wake up your soul, align your spirit, and ensure that nerves don't take control when you're in front of an audience. With this preparation, you'll be ready to share your message confidently and authentically. When you're prepared, grounded in your breath, and connected to your voice and body, you'll be ready to speak with clarity, conviction, authenticity, and presence. It is a way for you to connect so you can connect with your audience. Now you are ready to share your thoughts with the world!

7
Practicing Presence Connects the Mind, Body, and Soul

"If a man is to live, he must be all alive, body, soul, mind, heart, spirit."

— Thomas Merton, Thoughts in Solitude

Being present is all the rage these days, but when it comes to communicating, being in the moment can be difficult to achieve. Speakers are often thinking about so many other variables. If the stakes are high for a particular presentation, nervousness can pull a speaker out of the moment. Or they might be focused on the outcome versus what is actually happening in the room. The communicator could be thinking, will my listeners recommend me to others? Will they like the content of my presentation? Will they buy what I am selling? Using your five senses will allow you to combat these forces. Mindful use of sight, sound, smell, taste, and touch offers us a chance to observe the world in a way that heightens our artistic expression and allows us to be present in the moment, observant in the smallest detail, while continuing to connect with an audience.

When I was an acting student, one of our professors asked us to keep a daily sense memory journal. They wanted us to be students of the world, engaged, present, and connected to our emotions. He knew we didn't have much life experience (we were 18 years old), so he was setting us on a path for success to support us when creating the multifaceted characters we would be playing. The journal became a toolbox: we were remembering vivid memories and writing down emotional connections while experiencing the world with our senses. This sense memory exercise allowed us to refine our observational skills while at the same time experience something that we found to be interesting with one of our senses. By having us focus on sight, sound, smell, taste, and touch, we learned to observe the world in a way that was unique to each one of us. Being in tune with our senses, we were not thinking of other things, rather, we were in the moment, paying attention to the people around us, our emotions, and storing ideas for future projects in our journals.

When I start feeling disconnected from the moment, I use my senses to bring me back to the present in hopes of reconnecting my mind, body, and soul. For example, when I see flowers, especially zinnias, they bring me great joy, and this is how they affect my body through the senses:

Sight: Zinnias are bright and vary in color, unique in variety and size.

Smell: Some say they lack a noticeable scent, but I think they smell like spring.

Taste: They are bitter and taste like grass.

Sound: The ones I plant get very tall and make a

whooshing sound as they blow in the breeze.

Touch: The petals are smooth, but the stems are thick, rough, and they often make me itchy.

Zinnias remind me of my sweet paternal Grandma. In my mind I have vivid memories of her when I am working in the flower garden by my front porch. She was kind but firm, quiet but wise, sweet but strong, and she was a wonderful gardener. The memory of my grandma and her large vegetable garden with a zinnia at the front of each row makes my soul grateful. I sure did love her. The connection to my senses allows my imagination to kick in and has the potential to give me the impetus to create something new and wonderful.

Following the connection of my mind and body with my senses often elicits a powerful emotional response, thereby connecting the Trifecta. Living in the present moment gives us opportunities to be grateful, to imagine, to grow, to create, to observe the human condition without judgement. This kind of personal experience has the power to connect my mind, body, and soul.

You can see that just tapping into the senses using something that brings you joy can open up a world of emotions, memories, and bring you into the present moment. So, let's engage our senses right now—feel free to make notes in the margin or journal your experience. Let's start with sound. What do you hear around you right now? Is it music, a sound found in nature, or something as mundane as traffic?

Is there white noise such as a running furnace or air conditioner? How does what you're hearing make you feel? Does the sound or a specific song transport you to a different time and place? Do the sounds give you a memory or evoke an emotion? Jot your thoughts down. Before you move onto the next sense take a couple of three-dimensional breaths.

Smell is another powerful sense tied to mind and soul. Have you ever caught a scent that brought you back to a moment from childhood? Certain smells can evoke such strong memories that they transport us back in time. For instance, the smell of chlorine reminds me of my junior high days and it makes the hair on the back of my neck stand up. There were mean girls that bullied me and pushed me around in the hallway by the pool in my school. I have a full body reaction and go on high alert when I smell chlorine. On the flip side, when I smell freshly brewed coffee it brings me back to my maternal grandma's kitchen where she was always wanting to make her guests a meal (a trait that I definitely inherited). Some smells might cause a strong kinesthetic response in your body linking that particular smell to a memory, and an emotional response to that event. What do you smell right now? Is dinner cooking in a crockpot? A candle burning? Is there a smell of clean laundry in the house? Or does it smell stale? Does the smell remind you it is time to take a shower? Make note of what you currently smell. If you have an emotional response or soul connection to that memory, record it now.

THE SPEAKER'S TRIFECTA

Taste is a favorite sense of mine, particularly because of my love for cooking. In fact, I often think of meals I make for my family as art projects, with lots of colors, textures, shapes, and placement of the food on the plate. For me, sharing a meal is a way to connect with others, offering an opportunity to swap stories, share experiences and connect. There's something life-giving about gathering around a table. Bring your attention to the present moment. What taste do you notice in your mouth? Did you have a meal previously with a strong taste, such as garlic? Did you just brush your teeth? Are you drinking something as you read this or are you snacking on something? What does it taste like? Does it hold a past memory for you or is the taste you're experiencing something new? Make notes on your mind and soul connection to the embodiment of the sense of taste.

Touch is all about texture for me. Some fabrics bring me comfort, while others irritate me. The tactile experience of touching different textures can sometimes trigger a memory and with that memory there will be emotions that come up as well. Look up and notice what is near you right now. Feel everything within your reach. How does this book feel in your hands? Bring your attention to where you are sitting. What are the fabrics around you like? The upholstery of the furniture you are sitting or laying on? The hard smooth wood of a chair you are sitting in? Are you snuggled in your bed with a soft animal or blanket nearby? Your tactical reaction to how your environment feels against your body can change the way you respond in the moment and even affect the way you are taking in this exercise with touch. Does anything you touch trigger a surprising response in you? Make note of that now.

Last but not least is the sense of sight. In our digital age, we're constantly bombarded with visual information. Our eyes are often overwhelmed by images, advertisements, social media, pop-ups, and screens. We see but do we really "see?" When we intentionally focus on what we see around us, whether it's nature, art, or the people we love, our sense of sight has the ability to ground us and bring us into the present moment. However, when it comes to sight it is important to be specific. Look up and see the shapes, lines, colors, objects, shadows, light, and movement around you but avoid making a list of what you see. Choose an object to observe in detail. Where did it come from? Did you buy it? Was it given to you? Did you inherit the object from a family member? What is the color, shape, weight, and what is underneath? Set the object out of your sight-lines and write a detailed description of what you observed. Now go back and read what you wrote about the object. Is there anything to add? Does the object spark a memory, and did that memory or emotion come up for you in the moment or only upon reflection? Was the observation exercise an intellectual one or were you able to keep your mind, body, and soul connected in the moment? Make notes of how your sense of sight allows you to connect in the moment.

How do you feel after exploring your five senses? I hope you feel present and maybe you even discovered some old memories that you might be able to use in a future message or talk. Using your senses to be present taps into many emotions that are helpful for a communicator to process and apply to their work.

Another exercise you might like to try is one that I often used with my theatre students. I would have them cover their eyes with a blindfold and experience the secret items: a ziplock bag of coffee beans, bubble wrap, a sliced apple, tinfoil, bubbles, hand cream, a bell, a roll of tape, silly putty, coins in a glass jar, etc. They were to interact with each item using their senses of touching, tasting, smelling, and hearing. They would spend about 45 seconds with an object before passing it to the person next to them.

As they moved through their time with each of the objects, I would encourage the students to experience each item with their remaining four senses and allow their imagination to think about what the object looked like and what color it might be if their sight was activated. After the exercise I asked each of them to articulate and share which sense was the strongest and initiated a memory for them. Next I asked them to pay attention to the current emotion they were feeling at that moment because of that memory. The responses after the exercise were rich, the students so grounded in their senses that these memories brought them right into the present moment. I had one student become emotional tasting and smelling garlic because it reminded her of her large Italian family, big parties with lots of Italian food, and it made her realize how much she missed her loud, wonderful family. This was just one example of many where my students used their senses to activate mind, body and soul in the present moment.

For the students, the sense memory exercise allowed them to experience their senses (body), have it bring back memories or ignite imagination (mind), have an emotional response to what they were experiencing (soul), and to share what they discovered verbally in the classroom. The students were engaging their mind, body, and soul which allowed them to bring their whole self into the present moment with their scene partners. It is important for actors playing characters to do this, but it is even more important for communicators to access their whole self to communicate authentically in the spaces where they are invited to speak.

There are other exercises that I use to tap into the senses, and that encourage the participant to be in the present moment. The Beholding Walk allows the participant to take in the world with all senses activated at the same time rather than isolating individual senses. The goal is to behold the world around you using your five senses. It ignites the soul, bringing you into the present moment of experiencing the world with your five senses. It can also bring up a memory with an emotional connection, or give you ideas for stories, images, or moments you can use in your talks. Beholding is a beautiful way to practice presence and gratitude. In Richard Rohr's book, Just This, he invites the reader to shift their thinking to mindfulness over constant striving and he encourages us to let go of our endless quest for more by finding fulfillment in "just this" —the present moment. Rohr offers several meditations and practices, one of which he calls beholding. I have taken his exercise and expanded it for my clients to practice presence.

My clients would start by choosing a place to go for a walk. Any place will do but I recommend starting with a place you think you know well, like your neighborhood or a park nearby. Before the speakers begin, they need to connect to their three-dimensional breath. I then invite them to open their eyes, step across a line or threshold, with a journal in their hand, and observe the world around them with all of their senses for about 20-30 minutes as they walk. They can jot things down as they go. Once the silent walk is done and they return to their starting point, I ask them to choose one thing that stood out to them, encouraging them to activate their senses and their emotional connection. Then I ask them to free-write about what they beheld on their walk. Their observations might allow them to recall a personal story that would support their content. However, more than anything using your senses can foster a mind, body, and soul connection to happen which will allow them to connect more deeply with their audiences. When speakers are connected and present, they will connect.

This heightened awareness of the senses will not only bring you into the present moment, but it will also connect your Mind, Body, and Soul. The Speaker's Trifecta connection happens when you have prepared (mind), rehearsed (body), are excited about the content (soul), and come into the present moment (senses). Building up a keen awareness of your senses will allow you to be present, and give you more access to potential anecdotes, personal stories, and memories. These connections will allow you to prepare a talk that is mindful, soulful, and completely connected to your body, resulting in a much more authentic experience from the speaker to the audience.

8
Movement in the "Box"
"Knowing yourself is the beginning of all wisdom."

— *Aristotle*

Mindful movement is just as important for online presentations as it is for in-person communication. And our world is continually taking more and more advantage of the digital space. But even in the confines of a "Zoom Box," your mind, body, and soul has the potential to either make a powerful impact or fall flat. (I will be using the word Zoom for simplicity, but of course the same goes for Microsoft Teams, or Google Meet, or whatever platform you are using for online communications.) If you consider utilizing your space in an online presentation the way you would on a platform, this mindfulness will help you connect authentically with your audience—even through a computer screen. If your Zoom presentations are prepared with intention, your audience will connect with you. If you want to break through the digital barrier, prepare your whole self (mind, body, and soul). You should rehearse your content where you communicate online, warm-up your voice and body, connect to your three-dimensional breath, pay attention to your shaping and movement in the Zoom box, all in order to connect with the people you are speaking to online.

Much of our work today happens in online spaces, and it is up to you as the speaker to foster an environment of respect and focus where participants feel valued, heard, and understood. Establishing a healthy Zoom space requires the speaker to prioritize intentionality and look for ways to engage the attenders. At the start of your sessions with clients or colleagues, I would suggest that you share some of your expectations in the Zoom space so everyone in attendance engages in a mindful, honoring way.

Of course, sometimes it is difficult leading an online meeting because the digital nature of the meeting allows for more readily available distractions. It can be tempting to call out a lack of focus. But if you have done your job as a communicator to prepare, warm up, and connect, I would encourage you to assume the best of people. Trusting that they are with you is a great way to create a healthy virtual space. All of you are working towards a common goal, so "hold the space" for one another in the "box." Your preparation for the online meeting gives you the best chance to keep everyone engaged; they will have fewer opportunities to multitask, check emails, or send texts during your time together. Stay in the present moment! If you do, your attendees will connect and engage with you in the virtual space.

While you may not be able to enforce Zoom "rules" in your environment, offering guidance can improve the overall efficiency of a meeting. At the beginning of your presentation, consider setting up some expectations especially for people in your organization. Request that microphones are on mute unless you have a question or need clarification. You might even put some simple notes in the chat at the beginning of your meeting as encouragement. By using the chat, you are also going first to let them know that the chat room is available for questions, comments, and encouragement of one another as you move through the meeting. If there are groups of people at the office in the same room on the Zoom, please encourage them to keep conversations in the room to a minimum so that they don't become a distraction.

Another thing that I find to be incredibly important during Zoom meetings is having participants keep their cameras on so that we can see everyone in the "Box". Since the pandemic, we have fewer in-person meetings and gatherings and more Zoom meetings. Some have not returned to their offices after the pandemic and these online meetings are the only place where we are "seeing" one another. Be present with one another and treat people the way you would like to be treated in your organization's Zoom meetings. By keeping your cameras on you are extending courtesy to one another, showing respect for the person presenting content in the Zoom session.

Communicating content online can be fun, and if you are leading the meeting, find ways to make the delivery of content memorable. Use breakout rooms and structure interactive moments to give opportunities for levity and participation. Sometimes the Zoom meetings can stack up back-to-back, and in these cases, I strongly suggest that you implement and schedule "passing periods." Leave 7-10 minutes between Zoom meetings for yourself and others to reset, move, breathe, and prepare for the next task.

Encourage your team to do exactly that - by shifting physical positions, such as standing if you've been sitting, refreshing both mentally and physically. Give yourself time to prepare the content for your next meeting and allow for a mental gear shift. These online "passing periods" will be a gift to your whole organization, an opportunity to get ready for the next meeting whether it be on Zoom or in-person.

In the same way that a communicator will take in and prepare the platform they are presenting on, the space where you are holding your Zoom meeting should be mindfully considered. Whether it's your home or office, this space represents you and your organization. Make sure to create a professional virtual environment for everyone in the meeting through your consideration of these elements:

    1. Camera placement: Ensure your camera is on a flat, stable surface at eye level. This helps create a more personal and professional connection.

    2. Look into the camera: When speaking, look directly at the camera. Eye contact fosters a sense of engagement and authenticity with your audience. If you need to, place your notes and/or images of others near the placement of your camera on your computer

or phone so that it's easier to keep your eyes at camera level.

3. Framing: Position the top of your head near the top of the screen, with your sternum near the bottom. This creates a balanced and professional look.

4. Lighting: Use natural light, if possible, and ensure it's shining on your face. Avoid sitting with a window behind you, as this can create shadows and obscure your face.

5. Warm up: Do a brief vocal and physical warm up before your presentation and take a few moments to connect with your breath.

6. Stay connected, even while moving: If you need to step away from your computer momentarily, make sure you can still be heard. Having the right audio and video equipment is key to maintaining engagement without disruptions.

7. Listening posture: When others are speaking, find stillness so that your physical movements draw focus away from yourself, and toward the other person speaking.

8. Involve your colleagues: Before important Zoom meetings, ask for feedback on your setup. Colleagues can help you find the best angles, lighting, and backdrop. Treat your Zoom space like a mini movie set, refining every detail for maximum impact.

9. Keep breathing: Amidst the tech and the setup,

don't forget to breathe! Remaining calm and centered is essential for delivering a confident and impactful presentation.

By following these simple guidelines, you can create a Zoom environment that not only reflects your professionalism but also engages and connects with your audience on a deeper level. Remember, mindful movement and thoughtful preparation are just as important in a virtual space as they are on a physical stage. Your mind, body, and soul have just as much to communicate in the digital space as they do in the flesh—the Trifecta can have a significant impact on your leading and communicating, even online!

9
The Trifecta for Connected Communicators

"The single biggest problem in communication is the illusion that it has taken place."

— George Bernard Shaw

Our church teaching assessment team gathered in the theatre space waiting for our next speaker. We were going to be observing a new pastor, Ian, who had already been hired. As he came in and introduced himself, it seemed to me that he was a bit nervous, as the process of assessment can be intimidating, even when you've already "got the job." After he spoke, he received positive feedback on content, tone, and structure from other assessors in the room. But before they could give that feedback, I asked him a simple question: "Are you self-conscious about your height?" He later told me that question stopped him in his tracks. The question wasn't at all what he was expecting, and he didn't know at first how to answer. So I asked him again, "Are you self-conscious about your height?"

My question gave him pause because he had to admit that it was true. He was self-conscious about his height. What he couldn't understand was how I was able to perceive that from his presentation. How did I arrive at this conclusion?

His physical habits were communicating so much—everything he was doing physically was linked to insecurity about being shorter in stature. His hands were in his pockets, his back and torso were narrowing in shape, there was a repetitive shoulder shrugging habit, and his eyes were often focused on the ground. But even with all those habits present, he still spoke with utter authority, and the talk he delivered was full of power. I understood why he was hired—he was a great writer and teacher! And his mind and soul were completely connected... he just left his body behind. Prior to this assessment, Ian didn't think much about how the use of his body could support his content.

It wasn't until a few weeks later that he was able to articulate what he experienced when I asked him that question in his assessment. He told me he had been preaching for ten years, had attended classes, workshops, and conferences, and no one had ever identified any of the things that I observed while he was communicating. He was wondering: How has no one ever witnessed what I observed when he was speaking? Why was he hearing my feedback now for the first time? Over the next several years in our church, I saw him beginning to release the insecurities he held in his body. Slowly, bit by bit, I saw him mindfully taking time to find places to ground his feet and stop moving. He became more intentional about widening from side to side with his arms, taking opportunities to slow down, and connecting his upper and lower body. I witnessed him methodically and mindfully embody his content. Over time, the insecurities I initially observed in his movement began to shift. It was exciting to watch how mindful movement transformed the way he communicated.

The Speaker's Trifecta (mind, body, soul) is a blueprint to help speakers incorporate mindful movement into their presentations. Full integration of the Trifecta in every phase of development will allow you to craft your own personalized communications practice as you continue to move towards embodying your content authentically.

Integration can begin as early as the ideation phase for your content. Consider incorporating movement when writing. Whether it's taking a walk when you feel stuck, simply shifting from sitting to standing as you brainstorm, or speaking the words you have on paper out loud as you've written them. Moving in this phase can begin the embodiment process, which will help you stay connected to your breath and body. Keep mixing things up to keep your process fresh. Once your content has been written you will begin the process of moving internal intellectual content into external space with your body and voice.

Your first reading of your manuscript should be done out loud while standing. Record yourself on video to see what initial instincts you have for gestures or impulses to move in the space. Consider how you naturally move and what habits might be getting in the way. Watch your video back and make notes of your observations on your manuscript. Decide on a few more intentional choices for shaping, tempo, stillness, and use of stage space throughout your talk. Try these choices on and if your movement doesn't feel authentic, don't be afraid to let those choices go and try something different.

During the embodiment process, stay curious about yourself and your movement preferences. Notice physicality that repeats and pay attention to moments when you feel uncomfortable and moments when you feel grounded. Once you have settled on your physical choices, rehearse your talk at least two more times in full performance mode. Do not neglect the physical aspect of preparation. It's vital to rehearse on your feet so that you have an idea of the energy you will need to fill the space when speaking. Your body has knowledge and will utilize muscle memory to retain your movement choices from your rehearsal. Being embodied will allow you to connect to your audience in the moment and you won't be thinking about your movement choices.

Next, warm up physically, vocally, and connect to your three-dimensional breath before you step into the space. Make sure you are grounded and present in the moment. It's time to let go and trust your preparation. You can do it!

You are now prepared for your presentation! When practicing mindful movement, your body will tell the same story as your content. Your mindful preparation will set you apart as an excellent communicator. That being said, every now and then I still run into speakers that don't like to prepare.

They feel like it takes away their spontaneity. Some people ask me why they can't just wing their presentations, and "let the Spirit guide them." They feel like they have more freedom and consider themselves to be more "in the moment." My advice? **DO NOT WING IT!** This process does not remove any possibility of in-the-moment spontaneity. There will always be places where you can go off script or share something that occurs to you during your talk. You can share that extra anecdote or adapt to the responses of your audience because you have a structure to return to that has been rehearsed. These moments of spontaneity are better served when presented within a foundation of a manuscript or clear outline. You don't need to have it on stage with you if that throws you off, but good time management comes from that level of preparation.

You have been given a specific time frame to communicate your message. Respect your audience and the event organizers by staying within that limit. Your script, (including your personal stories) should take that timeframe into account, and wandering off-script over and over again will most likely cause you to run over time, disrupting the schedule of events. Another reason to prepare exactly what you are going to communicate is that it helps you maintain your focus of the talk, keeping the main thing, the main thing. Going off-script too often can lead to unplanned and unwanted tangents, adding random content, thereby losing the focus or high point of your presentation. Like any great story, your talk should have a clear beginning, middle, and end. *Note: this is just like a breath! You* **begin** *with an impulse to inhale, the* **middle** *is at the height of the inhalation just before the impulse to exhale, and the* **end** *is at the bottom of the exhale. Remember, breath is the impulse for movement in the body and voice.*

When rehearsing your talk, bear in mind the room in which you'll be delivering the message. If you are unfamiliar with the space, ask those who are to explain the room to you. Know your boundaries on the platform, ask about the size of the space, lighting, camera placements, whether you will have a table or music stand of some sort, and whether your preferred microphone will be available. It is also okay to ask for the things that you prefer, especially if they will allow you to communicate more effectively. Even understanding the size of the room will help you prepare to claim the space with your whole self and connect with your audience more effectively, giving yourself the opportunity to practice with the space in mind.

As you move from rehearsal to presentation, you can begin to experiment with the concepts outlined in this book. However, it is important to note that this is merely an introduction to the practices I regularly employ with my clients. If your curiosity has been sparked, I would love to be able to help you take the next steps in your development as an excellent communicator. Whether you're a speaker, teacher, pastor, doctor, lawyer, or executive—or simply someone looking to elevate your communication skills—I offer in-person and online workshops, classes, and 1:1 coaching to support you on your journey as a communicator. We have all had different lives, experiences, and events that affect our movement patterns. My coaching is personalized to the individual. We'll look at your speaking style, your preferences for movement, and learn together how your life story is reflected in your habits, acknowledging who you are without judgement.

We'll work to neutralize habits, use mindful movement to increase a physical vocabulary, and rediscover who you are in authentic voice and body. I trust that your journey as a communications athlete will be incredibly personal, eye-opening, and an embodied experience that will help you engage all three elements of *The Speaker's Trifecta: Mind, Body, Soul.* Reach out if you'd like to learn more. I'd love to hear from you!

ACKNOWLEDGEMENTS

Eric Bramlett, you are a saint! Thank you for encouraging me, being my sounding board, helping with editing, and for being so incredibly patient with me on my writing journey.

Kim Brown at Minerva Rising Press, my editor and friend, you have a brilliant mind. I appreciate you helping me clarify and structure my thoughts in this book.

To John Blumberg who told me I should be doing this work in the first place, thank you.

Dave Ferguson for embracing an artist and always leading with a yes. I am so grateful for you!

Columbia College Chicago Dance Movement Therapy Department (Creative Arts Therapy) instructors and professors who supported me as I earned my GL-CMA. I had no idea that certification would lead me into new spaces with communicators and change my career path.

My children, Sadie, Elijah, Dillon, Abby, and Anna Louise, who cheered me on during my writing process.

My parents, Jerry and Lois Vander Kooi who always made me think I could do anything if I put my mind to it! I love both of you dearly.

My brother and sister in law, David and Kaisa Vander Kooi, who let me use their home in Michigan for writing retreats at the beginning of my process.

The assessment team at Community Christian Church. Humbled that you asked me to serve in the assessment space. What I did there, led me where I am today.

Diane Bakker for getting me organized. It takes a lot of work to wrangle an artist. Thank you can't even describe how grateful I am for your heart to serve others.

Thanks to Danielle Strickland, Cheryl Nembhard, and the Women Speakers Collective who trusted me to share what I know about embodiment at many of their events: Bootcamps, PreacHER Academy, Story Strong, and Renew Retreat.

There were so many other people along the way cheering me on, giving me teaching opportunities, encouraging me, and hiring me. Their trust along the way showed me that what I was offering was something missing in training for communicators. Thank you, my friends!

Evan McBroom, Terri Saliba, Carrie Williams, Shawn Williams, Deb Walkemeyer, Beth Paz, Grace Aquilina, Ian Simpkins, Kadi Cole and Company, Melissa Mashburn, Janet McMahon, Brad Tate, Jennifer Pedley, Aubrey Sampson, Kelly Olson, Tammy Melchien, Sue Ferguson, Noemi Chavez, Chrissy Mayer, Amy Hafner, Sharon and Tim O'Neill, Ruth Lorensson, Melissa Mashburn, The Called Creatives-Alli Worthington and Lisa Whittle, Becky and David Stevenson, Keely Morley, Mindy Caliquire, Chicago Police Department, World Vision, Aspen Group, Generis, twoxfour agency, Ministry Chick, Exponential Conference, Youth for Christ, and all of my former students.

This book is dedicated to my Husband, William Eric Bramlett. He is the only one in the world who could get me to write a book.

Kristi Bramlett has spent over 30 years building a multifaceted career as a professional actress, college professor, mentor, coach, and Certified Movement Analyst, working with communicators around the world. Her passion for helping others connect authentically—with themselves, their audiences, and their content—has shaped her life and career.

Kristi specializes in helping communicators understand their unique movement preferences, expand their physical vocabulary beyond habitual patterns, and align their bodies with their message for greater impact. As a movement analyst, she equips speakers with tools to discover their authentic, connected self, ensuring that their presence and delivery match the power of their words.

Her expertise has led her to serve on the assessment team at Community Christian Church for more than a decade, supporting campus pastors, worship leaders, and teaching pastors. She has also partnered as an embodiment coach with numerous organizations, including Women Speakers Collective Bootcamps, Story Strong, Renew Retreat, PreacHER Academy, Stadia, Exponential, World Vision, Baton Pass, Generis, Ministry Chick, Willow Creek, and Aspen Group.

Kristi lives in Naperville, Illinois, with her wonderful husband, Eric, and treasures time with her amazing family. Passionate about faith, growth, and authentic connection, she continues to inspire communicators to engage audiences with confidence, presence, and heart.

www.ingramcontent.com/pod-product-compliance
Lightning Source LLC
Chambersburg PA
CBHW051607170426
43196CB00038B/2955